# The Temperature of This Water

# The Temperature of This Water

by Ishle Yi Park

Kaya Press

2nd printing, 2005

05   04   03   02

Published by Kaya Press
an imprint of Muae Publishing
www.kaya.com

Cover design by Purple Gate Design  www.purplegatedesign.com
Interior design and typesetting by Sandra Watanabe
Cover photo by N. Rain Noe

Manufactured in the United States of America

Distributed by D.A.P./Distributed Art Publishers
155 Avenue of the Americas, 2nd Floor
New York, NY 10013
(800) 338–BOOK  www.artbook.com

ISBN 1-885030-39-8
Library of Congress Catalog Card Number: 2004103649

This publication is made possible with public funds from the New York State
Council on the Arts, a state agency, as well as the JPMorgan Chase SMARTS
Regrant Program and the Asian American Arts Alliance, the Lower Manhattan
Cultural Council, Soo Kyung Kim, Wook Hun and Sun Hee Koo, Eileen Tabios,
Ronald and Susan Yanagihara, and many others.

State of the Arts

NYSCA

FOR UMA, APA, and SUNWOO

# CONTENTS

## Turtles

This is a story about two people
searching for a home. No. This is a story
about a country searching for a home —

liberation fighters spilling blood
to speak their own words, whole as moon-dusted
pears weighing down orchards. Farmers beating
hourglass drums on dirt, cracking their throats
and sweatriver backs to call this land Chosun. Son.

My father grew up barefoot, eating robins' eggs,
ripping skins off trees, kicking a leather rugby ball, prying open
a locked door to get at candy and toy trucks
the GIs left his father.

My mother also grew up chasing army trucks
for bubble gum and trinkets,
until she realized some things are not
worth chasing. For bending into dust.

But they bent for each other —
in dust, in drinks, with handwritten letters
in a language I must mouthe to read,
their words forming calligrams of love.
No. This is not romantic.

These are my parents, running
with students, rioting and beaten,
tanks riding bareback through Seoul.
This is about my father, waiting tables at Friendly's,

sloppy and loose-tongued, the other whiteboy waiters
laughing at his flustered mouth.

This is about my mother, picking thorns
off roses in a factory with her sister,
her fingertips scarred and bleeding.

This is about her sister,
who brought them over by marrying
a white soldier who became crazy,
then a family secret.

Breaking bones of mackerel.
Croaker. Over the dinner table.
Breaking each other. Bruised rib,
scarred elbow. Twenty-five years of
selling fish. Breaking backs. Promises.

This is about a daughter.
With a suitcase packed with Wise onion chips
and a moth-eaten blanket. Typing fourth-grade runaway letters.
Staring into her rice,
kimchee flung, guksu spilt, bowl chipped —
thrown. Girl, curled in bunk bed.

Girl grown.
Trying to find home in wild asphalt rhythms,
a bleeding, copter-scarred sky.
Headlights and searchlights and strobelights
and him. Wire-thin, carved.
His eyes swallowed her whole.

He was beauty. He split her skin,
kissed her hip bones, bruised her jaw.
She pried him open, searched the chords of his hair,
listened to the clave of his heart, punched his chest. Tried to leave.

Dragged him across carpet,
his arms a bracelet around her ankles.
He refused to let go of his only home.
And she began to see: how we cling to fragile walls,
dilapidated roofs, rib-like planks, knobby floorboards,
this first home/body pounded and grown out of necessity,
love. Biting love. Survival love.

The daughter looked back.
At her. At him. Calloused. Apron-stained. Graying.
And she began to cry.
For them,
her country.
Ravished, split, clawing.
        All for home.
            And began to love
                this leatherbacked thing she called a heart.

We live by waters breaking out of the heart.

— Anne Carson

## 1977

Besides being the year I was born,
my parents remember it
as the opening of Utopia Fishery,
apa scotch-taping his first
hand-drawn sign
to the glass window.

Others say it was the year of
New York's blackout, when
other fathers stole whole
mattresses from Sealys
on Knickerbocker and Myrtle.

Still others are quick to mention
Elvis and his sad demise,
conspiracy theories and
the double entendre of 7–7,
amateur numerologists
practicing illuminati
decades before their time.

I mark this: strange rhythm
of years that still excites me,
makes me wonder about death,
my mother's ears, and the shape
of her waist before I was born,
nights she spent drinking shots
of soju in Daegu bars,
building mud huts on Surak-san,

before homework and recitals
and cooking three meals
burdened her days
before 2nd grade
before American capitalist tooth fairies
before fist fights
before me.

To my mother, Easter is
another fish-eating holiday —
long-drawn Fridays
sticking her arm in the lobster tank,
cutting strips of grey "lemon sole,"
the smell of rotten pisser clams
funkifying behind the register,
its constant cha-ching never exceeding four digits,
the monotony of handling singles.

My mother, a constant blur
caught in awkward stills —
hands in air flipping on Chico,
fingers sifting deftly through bills,
nails splitting jang jo lim, dark meat
torn in strips, lips pulling smoke
from Kent 100's,
nights she lies on the living-room couch
with no pillow, stiller than white sky,
stiller than butterflies at rest.

## Anatomy of a Fish Store

Let me tell you about Suja. She is the real owner of
Utopia Fishery. All the business is conducted in her black and
white composition notebook, on a big-ass calculator (Texas
Instruments too complicated, numbers too small to see without
glasses), and in her head. She has two children raised in the
States, one a natural childbirth, the other pulled out against
her will by a Roosevelt Hospital doctor who used her as an
experiment for his students because she couldn't speak English.
President of her class in high school, graduate  of Seoul
University with a degree in English, she reads *Beloved* at night
after she does the bills on the flat kitchen table, when the
house is asleep and there is no one up to bother her. She
smokes Kent 100's in closets and basements and empty cars.
Her hands heal; she has healing hands. Here, in the back of the
fish store, by the oven and the food, her husband occasionally
beats her in front of the workers.

Suja's husband, Jong Suk, is the official owner of the fish
store. His name used to be splashed across sports pages every
Sunday in Korea; he was a national rugby star, and most people
back home know who he is. He drew all the posters and the
handmade fish paintings taped up to the window. At parties, he
is a hit, best karaoke singer, loud voice, good hwatoh player.
Customers hate him for being so loud. He does not drink,

smoke, or gamble. He drives to Fulton every morning at three to pick up fresh fish, has done so for the past twenty-five years. He and his wife are currently not talking. He cannot talk to his son, but is trying. Really trying.

His son Seung Ho just scored 1400 on his SAT's without even trying, without even going to school for the past two years. He sent out his college apps yesterday. He is currently on five years probation for crimes committed while he was part of GS, a Chinese gang. As a child, he was always being shut up or cut off. Victor down the block used to sic a German shepherd on him every time he ran down the street. Once, a group of twelve white boys jumped him in front of their house, banged his head into the back bumper of their green Impala. They took turns spitting big wads into his face and calling him a chink. Suja went to this house to defend her son, and the parents of the white boys would not let her on the porch. They threatened to let loose their rottweiler if she did not get off their property. Seung calls himself a chink now, jokingly, with his Chinese friends, and he does not run down these hateful blocks anymore — he walks like he owns them.

Let me tell you about Nick. You think he is the owner of the fish store. He talks to you about Italy and the good old days, even though he has never been there. He gives discounts to policemen and firemen; he talks about black people as "those animals" and hates working for "Chinese." He thinks

Giuliani is God's gift to the world. All his sentences begin with "my wife" and end with a sigh and "what can you do." If you don't know him, he is very charming actually. He is a good foot taller than the rest of us who work in the store. He takes more coffee and lunch breaks than anybody else. He looks very nice, a distinguished old gentleman. He is a necessary evil.

Chino makes all of Nick's food; in fact, he takes care of all the cooking, plus the thousand-dollar orders at Christmas. Without him, the store wouldn't run. He can jump two feet to knock a pot off the shelf and can kill an eel with his bare hands. He makes elaborate and beautiful lobster plates, and shrimp cocktails with slices of lemon and sprigs of green parsley; in some other world, he would have been an artist. He almost died crossing the border to come here ten years ago, had to pay $800. Every Saturday night, he goes out dancing after work with Matute, telling us about his different girlfriends the following Monday. He has a wife, two kids, and a bright blue Camaro. He calls Suja *suegra*, Spanish for mother-in-law. He often fights with Jong Suk, and one of them won't show up at work for days, usually Jong Suk. They both think they are the boss. There is much I don't know about Chino.

Matute is my mother's pet. He also calls her *suegra*, calls me *mi amor.* He is eighteen, works two jobs, 12 hours a day, 6 days a week, lives in a small apartment in Yonkers with three other people he doesn't know. He had to pay $4,000 to get here, paid it all off in the first working month. He married some woman to get a license at the courthouse: he wore a rented tux, and she, 40 years old, showed up in sweatpants and t-shirt, her hair in a ponytail. When business is slow, we dance bachata on the wet tiles in the kitchen. My father doesn't like that Matute doesn't work when I am around, so Matute cooks in the back mostly, frying flounder, shrimp, and crab cakes; I'm in the front.

Then there's Leo, currently engaged in a little love affair with Jesenia, the 19-year-old part-time worker we lured from McDonalds. He slices fish bodies, cuts up eels, carves clams from their shells, and does all the packing. He wears big boots, carries a knife, rarely talks, and smiles wide. Chino jokes about all the gay customers who have come in and hit on Leo. Leo talks to me about politics and race while eating rice near the garbage bins over lunch. How I should never marry a Korean, how Salvadoran men are more gentle. We have debates. He has seen my mother getting beaten in the back. Many things we leave unspoken.

Let me tell you about me. I am Suja's daughter, Jong Suk's daughter, Seung's sister, Nick's nemesis, and, according to Chino, his second wife. I work the cash register on good days, peel shrimp on slow ones. I am usually never here, only on days like today. Valentine Day's weekend always pulls in a small crowd, two lobsters and a bunch of shrimp for everybody. I was born and raised in Queens, but my mother has sent me away, almost pushed me out that door to Sweden, Cuba, Jamaica. Anywhere and everywhere to get out of here, to see with my eyes the places she always wanted to. *Go*, she says. I am a fish-store owner's daughter. Chino says I am spoiled. Maybe he's right, but I love my parents fiercely, even my father, and we come together to face customers like you.

Let me tell you about you. You come in here with your fingernails gleaming and outstretched; you've just had them done next door at ajumma's beauty salon. My mother is jealous of your nails, not because she likes them, but because you have the time to do them. You have more make-up on your face this Wednesday afternoon than my mother would wear in a whole month — you are two years younger than her but look ten years older. You wrinkle your nose at the stench we work in. You say hello to Nick, of course; he compliments your beauty, the new coat. You ask him how business is doing. He talks like he is the owner. Nick goes in the back for his lunch; then you bother my father. It is clear that you don't like each other. You haggle about the price (*Last week they were $11.99 a pound, weren't they?*), make him stick his arm in the freezing tank about twenty times until he gets two lobsters that are just the right size, and I ring you up. For some reason, you notice me for the first time. *Oh, Suzy,* (you call my mother by the wrong name), *is this your daughter?* She says yes, and you proceed to talk about me as if I weren't there — *She's so cute, she looks just like you.* You are surprised to hear I go to college. You say you should go now. Your chauffeured sedan is waiting. You wait for my brother to carry the lobster that you can't bear to hold, the lobster you will supposedly cook for dinner. You can't stand them when they look so alive like that. They scare you.

Seung walks you to your car, holding your bags. *Put them on the floor,* you order, and since you're feeling generous, you palm him a dollar tip. You leave, and life goes on. You are one of 76 customers a day, 237 a week; not the worst, not the best.

Inside, business goes on as normal. Fish are racked and stored in trays in the freezer, shelves are emptied of their ice. There are more important matters at hand — what needs to be ordered — salmon? halibut? little neck clams? For Chino, it's whether my father will give him a $2 raise, or if he has to threaten him by working in the seafood section of Key Food again. For my father, it's who will take over the store when he retires — Leo or Nick? Never mind that — my mother worries how long we can last, with her son in a gang and her husband scaring away the old customers. Plus, she counts three shrimp platters and two crates of king crab legs missing; she can't fire anyone, but wants to know who is to blame. Matute is spraying Brut cologne over the sweater he'd carefully packed away in the green bathroom; tonight he is going to pay older

Ecuadorian and Mexican ladies $2 to dance with him in
Yonkers. He straightens his jacket collar in the dirty mirror.
Leo locks up, brings down the iron grill with a metallic shudder
and slam.

   My father leaves early with me. I am thinking about
a shower, a boy, and Cuba, about the forced conversation I
will share in the van with my father, how I will spend most
of the ride staring out the passenger seat window. I confess: it
is easy for me to leave. Once in a while I have a fish dream,
but I wake up.

   This is Utopia Fishery. It stands between Gino's Italian
Restaurant and Joey's Pet Shop in a small mall in Yonkers that
includes a Rite Aid, a bank, a bagel shop, a nail salon, and
McDonalds. Behind it, a sheer cliff carved into rock falls into a
clump of dilapidated metal garbage tanks. No rats, maybe a few
mice, a few black droppings as evidence. In front, an empty
parking lot of asphalt and white grids, small pools of light from
the high lampposts. On the sides, haggard graffiti on brick,
names tagged and crossed out in black spray paint. Inside, a
metal freezer stacked with mackerel, eel, kimchee, 2-liter
Cokes, clams oreganata in aluminum pockets, six to a box,
sprinkled with hot pepper, and wooden crates of unmarked fish
lying with one dead eye up. Inside: a frozen heart, stocked and
emptied every day. Inside: a dark, constant hum.

## Pine-Wood Uncle

My uncle makes a living out of his van,
out of pine wood he fits together with callused hands,
hands that picked locks at the age of five
in a small Korean province
until, collar-dragged home, storeowners
demanded to know which gangsters
he was working for.

Not afraid of death, he drinks
cheap soju and once
punched his wife
while we trawled toy truck
underfoot on carpet, already fixed
to ignore the war around us.

Once slashed his own
tight stomach like a mouth
and readied the blade again
for his brother-in-law, blood curling
down the sink.

He sobs old love songs
in the next room, wall a curtain
muffling his drunk dance,
while his son, under cover of a cotton blanket,
wills his father to love him
or die, die, die.

## What I Did When My Man Got Stabbed

I did not walk him down two flights
or sit with him on Knickerbocker's curb
under the dirt haze of August sun
until the ambulance,
two hours late, pulled up.

I stood in the kitchen with Maritza,
eight-months pregnant, serrated steak knife shaking,
as she talked about killing herself
in front of me.

*Maritza, put down the knife,* I cooed,
until she clattered it
into the sink of plastic bowl
and Mickey Mouse cup,
sunk into the chair. I dropped

next to her, leaned into her face,
even smoothed her pulled hair,
got her a cup of Pepsi she fingered
but did not sip, said *sorry, Mari, sorry,*
even though ten minutes before we'd stood so close

we smelled each other, I about to punch her,
regardless of the baby. I picked up the tissue paper
crumpled like white blossoms around her new
queen bed, the one her brother and I laid in,
spreadeagled after sex,

how she found us, passed out, half-dressed.
Four Coronas on the linoleum. I picked up
the tissue. Pulled the t-shirts half thrown out the window
back in, folded them. We walked outside,
sun blinding. Called hospitals from pay phones
to find him. A lot of young men stabbed that Sunday.
Split cab fare. She sat outside, scared.
I touched him, lying limp on the stretcher,
and he turned away.

She wanted to be the first to bless
that bed. The one she paid $200 for.
We sat on cold granite seats outside Bellevue Hospital
and talked like sisters. I never saw her again.

Later, I went to visit him with flowers.
*I'm not dead yet*, he frowned, and we watched
the hanging tv, our bodies reflected in the window
against the skyline.

## Meat Trucks

*When I cannot look at your face,*
I look at your back
curled away from me in sleep,
half buried in polyester sheets.

I know it supports you
under wooden crates of packed beef
hauled off loading trucks
on lamplit streets. It's almost geometric
in its tight bend, hoist, pull
that cranks you through the mornings.

In these strange lights,
its ridges are reptilian and fierce,
but when my fingers graze your spine,
it shudders like a quiet earthquake.

## Uma's Advice

*keep licking his ass*

holes in walls and the gnashing of teeth
Heinekins in the long grass

what rests behind pink eyelids

(motherfucker you are my one and only)

he sits in a corner
and bums over a song

she cuts stalks of hot kimchee
and sometimes her palm

(you are my voice
and my voice is you)

her fingers love sweet rice cake
and baby hair

*worst thing in the world*
*is a dumpling with no meat*

(why don't you stop banging on that door
and let me pee in peace?)

her mother, laughing now,
licks the air

## Fort Totten

My grandfather pulls me close to him on the sofa. He
smells like old people, but minty also, like mercury balls and
Vicks. His knuckles are huge and arthritic, four of them taped
over with white bandages. *Issilah*, he croaks in Korean. *Promise
me one thing.* Yes, I say, suspicious, *What? Promise me you will
only marry Korean. This is my dying wish.* He is solemn, with his
gummy face and pleated eyelids, but the old man is slick; he
knows what he's doing. *Yes*, I sigh. *I promise.* My father, chewing
a ragged string of squid on the floor and watching the Mets
game, smiles. *I hear you*, he calls. *Ayu, apa*, I groan, and shove
on my Nikes. *I'm going out.*

Little waits for me at the bottom of the hill. I can't
have my emo see him while throwing out the trash or watering
her window plants. We take the bus to Fort Totten and sit on
graffiti-chalked rocks, watching the sun lap over water and old
Chinese fisherman with dented buckets, listening to the foot-
long rats scurrying through dropped Budweiser cans.

We try to come here as often as possible. The Throggs
Neck Bridge is a blue necklace at this time of day, almost
blending into the horizon of water and sky.

Walking to Little's apartment in Bushwick means a
regular chorus of *pssst china, psst chinitas* for me, girls brushing
me on purpose as they pass by. Flushing is a bunch of leathery

Chinese men in paint-splattered jeans staring at Little to start a war, staring at me to make me feel dirty.

When something happens, like a girl sucking her teeth at us on the L train, or a man wanting to pick a fight, we head for the beach. Or Flushing Meadow Park. Or here — Fort Totten. Not even on purpose, I think. Our bodies just need respite, open space where strangers are not within two feet. Where we can lay on each other and be a couple, undisturbed, a clear forcefield around us blurring the sharp stares, teeth sucks, whispers.

*

Little is currently residing on his cousin Evette's couch, has been there for the past two months. It's been our bed, our refuge, our boxing ring. Outside, the Dominican sisters on the stoop, fanning their necks.

One night, we are arguing in the kitchen when Evette calls from work. I'm growling at him, spitting words like my father does to my mother — they shoot out of my mouth like lead bullets. We're still going at it, though he's on the phone with her. All of a sudden, she interrupts: *Bitch, who you think you are yelling at my cousin? With your Chinese ass. Can't even talk, ching chong ching chong ching.* I hear her through the phone as Little sits there in the kitchen. *What?* I spit, *What? You heard me,* her tinny voice shouts, louder, through the phone's small receiver. *Ching chong chink.* Little stays silent. I stand there, hands open and limp, unbelieving. She keeps hollering. I pick up my bookbag and stuff my clothes in, grab my coat. Then he hangs up the phone. Only then.

I'm so burnt I can't even think. *You tell that bitch to go fuck her dumb-ass self. Fucking ignorant bitch. Fucking half-Cuban Chinese, Puerto Rican bitch don't even see that she's insulting herself?!* Little is grabbing my arms, trying to calm me down. But I push him off, too disgusted to even punch him.

I sink into a tight square between the wooden bureau and the twin bed, and I don't even know how I start crying. The room is crazy messy, rugby shirts hanging off the backs of chairs, tissues on the floor, a few roaches in an ashtray by the open windowsill. Out in the alley, a man yelling. I can't breathe. I feel small, ugly, and ripped — a punctured balloon inside me, tattered plastic, no air.

For Little, who stayed silent. For Evette, making those noises, hating me, hating herself. And for me, cursing everything. *It was all a lie,* I say, *us driving to cop dimes off Myrtle, staying up to watch Showtime with a sixpack of Coronas, going to the Queens Day parade together. Bullshit. When it comes down to it, you're her cousin, and I'll always be the chink you're with.*

Little is silent, listening. And he will stay silent, because he is afraid to talk back to her, to defend me. *And that,* I spit, *is the biggest disappointment. I always thought you'd have my back. Fuck you, fuck her, fuck this, fuck you, fuck us.*

Little blocks the doorway. The lights are out, and all I see are his wide, remorseful eyes. I don't want to look at them, I'm tired of crying. And I don't want to touch him, I don't want to fight. I just stand in front of him, Jansport in hand, waiting to leave.

He tries to hug me; I shrug him off. He tries again; I slip under every time. *Get the fuck off,* I spit. *You coward.* He backs off, eyes wet. And he says, softly, *What about me? I can't even meet your family. You can't even bring me home.*

He stares at me in the shadowed kitchen. I look away, watch a roach crawl calmly over the lip of a plate. *That's not fair,* I say. *They wouldn't let me bring any guy . . .*

*Yeah,* he says quietly.

*You know how my father is,* I start again.

*I know,* he says.

I glance up at Little, but in my head, I'm back to last Friday in Flushing, when we had taken the 7 train back from the city. The subway was crowded and muggy, bookbags shoved up against my spine. It was a relief to walk up Roosevelt, air cool, hugging each other. We were halfway up the block, past the pizza shop, and Little had me in an affectionate headlock.

In front of me, dangling car keys in shorts and sandals, stood my speechless father. Little offered his hand. My father stared at it for a full minute like it was rotten. I didn't say a word. Something was abandoned there on the corner of

Roosevelt and Union, some trust between Little and me. My father and I left. In two years, it was the only time they had ever met.

*Is that how you act in the street?* My father had hissed in the shadowed van. My hands were shaking, I could only look in my lap. I blurted, *At least you could shake his hand! You couldn't even shake his hand.*

*I'm not racist,* he'd said to nobody. *I don't care he's black.* *Puerto Rican,* I spat. *Black, Puerto Rican, whatever. I don't care about anything color,* he continued. *Yeah,* I'd mumbled. *Whatever.*

Remembering this, my arm goes limp and I drop the Jansport on the kitchen linoleum. *I'm so tired,* I say. I want Little to hold me, but I can't say it. *Me too,* he replies. He wipes my chin slowly and I don't stop him. I lean into his palm and kiss it; he pulls me into him. And that's all I want.

*

The blue of the sky, the water, the beaded necklace of the Throggs Neck Bridge blend into each other. The water by our feet glints, lightly slapping the rock. Around us, the fishermen are staring seaward. A thin mother watches her child jumping cautiously on the rocks. Little touches a smooth stone etched with names: Josephine and Anthony, 1982 — forever. I lean back on him. *This is what I want,* I say, hugging his knees. He is seated behind me; I am between his legs. *What?* he asks. *What?* We both look out into the falling night, the indistinguishable horizon.

## uma haiku

My mother circles
want ads in the kitchen. Smiles.
Like that, she breaks me.

## Jejudo Dreams

In Jejudo, there are women who have dived for generations,
scalloping shells off coral reefs
to support their weak, spendthrift husbands
and sustain the island life. These women,
seal smooth with black river hair tied thick
into a bun, will, even nine months pregnant,
hold their breath and submerge.

In Queens, I read about them
as if they were not a part of my mother's memory,
as if she never once loved their indecipherable accents
thick with the knowledge of water
in a time when wet laundry still slapped on rock —
they skirted her Daegu reality.

I'm drowning in the land to which she swam,
and when I try to speak my language, my tongue
flops in my mouth like a dying fish:
desperate, silver, and shining with effort.
These fish line my parents' store shelves,
invade our dreams in huge, peeled-skin schools,
their sour, two-day old smell clings to my mother's
woolen sweaters and my father's corduroy pants,
to the dusk of their skin as they watch television.

This smell was my shame growing up,
my secret; the reason I took three showers a day,
got dropped off a block away from school
so the Whitestone kids would never know
that my father drove the puke-green van

smelling of fish, so they would never wrinkle
their noses at me and say I smelled like fish,
or dirty women. For fifteen years, I crossed my legs,
washed, prayed, hid.

I erased my mother's memories
and replaced them with rote school texts,
learned to be ashamed of my parents,
their accent, to interpret their hard-earned smell
as stink, to think diamond-cut eyes undesirable,
some of us trying to Anglicize them
with Elmer's glue or cosmetic surgery . . .

My dongsengs: what are we doing if not quietly, desperately drowning?
Who is here to teach us how to swim?

I want to know those Jejudo women
beyond their slick, oceanic fame —
if pollution from Seoul mars their skin,
    if broken shells shrapnel their callused palms,
        if their thighs are as smooth and tight
            as taut silk, if their hair ever danced
                with locks of fresh seaweed,
                    like the lyrics of songs they sing after work,
                        lyrics of songs they hear underwater,
                    if their husbands ever beat them,
                how they cry, how they laugh,
                    how they fight,
                        the mottled, murky bayous and lagoons
                        of their dreams.

How it feels . . . to hold your breath so long
your lungs, on the verge of bursting, steel themselves
while you grab, wrench that thing you need more than air,
and break surface.

There are times when I trivialize these desires,
but at night, I wonder: will my ancestors not hear me when I die?
Will they mistake me for a white bakwai ghost
because of my accent? Will all the history I embody
unravel with my time because this tongue
cannot recall the words braided into my bloodline?

These women, who are my women,
        these songs, which are my songs . . .

In Jejudo, there are women
who have dived for generations,

        they are calling me back to myself,
            the truest, rough coral of myself,

        I take a deep breath —

            and I go fish.

1. Wherever
2. I
3. go
4. I carry the sorrow of my country
5. its memory of water

— Eric Gamalinda

**City**

1.

we have become
a city of skittish colts
hooves on iron

fumes rise like
distended grief

dreams involve
the sound of glass

diffused and minimal
levels of light

2.

there are windows

    blast of mares

        teeth

          water

        all God

I have watched        loved

            wild

           crescent

           gutted

                    thirsting

with
no words
for all the wars
inside me

## Samchun in the Grocery Store

Last night I walked into a grocery store on East 3rd and Avenue B,
shocked by my uncle's face behind the counter:
*Issilah!* he smiled, with a broad sweep of arm,
*Take anything!* in this store that wasn't even his.

I wander a labyrinth of stacked aisles,
smell of orange yam meat roasting dark
and sweet as the sight of my samchun: dirty Mets cap,
chipped front tooth, crescent-moon eyes spilling light
over his rough beach of brown skin:

this samchun, who taught me to crack open warm walnuts
with my teeth, back cracked from hauling fish-store crate
and fruit carton, spine held stiff with a leather safety belt.

My samchun, hands exploding knife-into-fist,
telling my father: *if you ever hit that woman again
I chop off both your hands, like this —*

Samchun. After 26 years, just recently blessed
with a fat-cheeked granddaughter
whose Yi family earlobes
turn up like little buttons . . .

A customer enters. Grabs a Hershey bar,
a Heinekin, a pack of Lucky Strike cigarettes.
Asks, *How much is this? What? How much? Speak English!*

*1.19 . . . 1.19 . . . 1.19*, I hiss from behind the rack of Wise chips,
lemonade chilling my palms. I watch a mask eclipse
my samchun's face as he swallows the spit insults,
the go-home-chink, speak-English bullshit,
clicked trigger and bullet: I imagine him falling,
snapped neck under cigarette shelves. Fallen,

crushed flower at an altar of jagged store windows,
white picket signs, white arm bands,
Latasha Harlins, Soon Ja Du: thick blood
pooling on both sides of the counter . . .

I want to run up and bitch slap the man
for disrespecting my uncle, but this is not my battle;
this is just his job.

Somewhere, La India streams out an open car window.
Samchun rubs his temples. The customer slaps
silver change on the counter and leaves. Solitude freezes
this store trimmed with icicles and wet, black snow.

Suddenly I know why my love is a clenched fist,
why I can only love like this.
Samchun bags my Countrytime Lemonade
and tells me to watch it. Music outside
trails off like torn ribbon —
we hug over the dividing counter
as if our lives depend on it.

## Marine Rules
~ for David

Don't shoot a parachuter in air, but paratroopers are fair game.
When you capture a P.O.W., follow the 6 s's: *search secure silence
segregate safeguard and speed them to the rear.*

Stick together against Army & Navy punks.
Bless equipment men and commanding officers with bigger plates
      at mess hall.
Smoke only in steam-filled showers.
Wash at least twice a week; *pay particular attention to body creases.*

Don't turn your head at "Yankee, go home."
Don't think about your girl getting her back dug out by the next
      man in Queens,
don't remember your titi Margie cooking up a pot of fried wings
      for your departure,
how you both cried for an hour at her kitchen table.

Memorize Biggie's *Ready to Die,* unlike the rosaries you always forgot,
along with *this is my rifle, there are many like it, but only this one is mine,*
along with the dirt-hill chant, *'57 Chevy with a tankful of gas,
got a mouthful of pussy and a handful of ass. Sound off — one . . . two.
Sound off — three . . . four. Sound off — one . . . two . . . three . . . four . . .*

Remember — it matters where you die. In combat, a hero; in Brooklyn,
      a statistic.
Stop waiting for her letters, which grow scarcer than war rations.
Don't give a fuck about no one cuz they don't give a fuck about you —

Fuck the sergeant's wife on Guantanamo Beach,
remember her thick haunches against wet rock, the crashing foam,
    the darkness . . .
Don't cry where they can see you. *Don't give up don't give up don't*
    *give up* —
just two more years — do not go home a punk . . .

Remember you are an American fighting man: amphibious force-in-
    readiness,
the word *marine,* coming from the Latin *marinus,* meaning "related
    to the sea," *amphibious* from the Greek *amphibion,* literally,
    "living a double life."
Name things exactly — Civilian. Combatant. Officer. Wife. Man.
    P.O.W. Enemy.

**Horses**

winter
did I mention frost

my head is cold
my teeth whinny

and stomp in the stall
of my mouth

my skin is a frail barn
shivering in a ghostfield

in mountains
no one remembers

the wood itself is shivering

the horses grind
against each other

for warmth
chew at the leather

no fingers to dart
like woodmice

through the gone hay
and fine grain

no one to unlock
my unthawed hinges

crack icicles off the lip
of the slanted roof no one

to brush the horsetails
and the snow has eaten

all memory of the wheeled road
that once rutted itself

right to the door
of this thin-walled barn

### Saewoomtuh Flower Shop

Camp Casey Military Base, Tongduchon, Korea (August 2000)

Sung Mee curls a crepe rose petal with the blunt end of
scissors held like a joint or cigarette: she rolls a leaf to a
wire stem with green tape. An older ajumma says, *It's okay
to photograph the paper bouquets, but not the girls.*

My hands try to copy their petal-over-petal work, folds that can
be pulled, stretched, tucked as needed. *People grow tired of cheap
trinkets*, ajumma complains. *Please buy each flower you make for
500 won.*

*You look like a gangster*, Sung Mee frowns. *Let me do you over.* I
put down my rosebud, puckered like an old woman's lips.
Fingers resting on my temple, she rubs off my brows with spit,
paints the curve of an egg over each eye. This close, I see her
forearm laced with a patchwork of scars. We sit, stilled, her
hand resting on my cheekbone for a minute. Women nod *yes,
better.* Colored flakes lie strewn across the tiles. On the table,
scattered daisies, yellow orchid.

Ajumma sweeps glitter, crumpled tissue into a heap by the
belled door.

We leave our mistakes everywhere.

## Rikers

*I got called to the dance floor this morning. No time to shave, but at least got out before lockdown.*

This morning you walked towards me, one broken sandal, face unshaven. Leaning over to hug my thick arms.

*You looked good, girl. Don't think I didn't notice. Red bodysuit, my earrings, new haircut. Don't think it didn't hurt to see you así.*

We sit in those orange, kindergarten-sized plastic chairs. Couldn't move the table, COs said.

I'm so glad I didn't wear a skirt so I can spread my legs wider, our knees making a diamond under the table. My body is curved towards yours. I don't care where my stomach is.

*You told me about my pops, my sister, my brother. I told you about the dreads, the Puerto Rican who hides Aaliyah pictures under his bed, and Angie, the pata who rubs her new titties on the bars of our cell. She has this magazine, you know. Transsexual magazine that gives you the low-down on all the operations. Pictures too, before & after.*

Listen. I have to tell you something.

Last Tuesday, after court, your lawyer offered to buy me coffee, and over coffee, he said, "Nelson's a good kid, but . . . " and followed me on the train, telling me how he was gonna divorce his fat wife cuz things weren't working out, and you know how he talks a hundred miles an hour, he went from my wife to my back to can you give me a massage? Right there on the crowded #6, offering me his grey, polyester-suited back.

I had to tell you that, but some skin under your eyes and the angle of your head tells me, no. Not now. So I keep saying Listen. Listen. Listen.

*Listen? What, listen? I can't even hear myself think. I have to PUSH the air to breathe, ma. Twelve bunks to one cell, c'mon now. Least I have the dreads to keep Angie from gettin' fresh, but you never know. Last night I spent two hours carving your name into an Ivory bar to calm me down. I dyed the letters with black. Ink from postage. Brown background with coffee. Made it look rough and scratched, like dark mountains. And the red heart in the corner, ma? Colored with stolen Jello. You gotta see it. It's phat. To calm me down. Cuz I realized. I sat there watching Mr. G. every night like a fool, keeping track of weather I can't see. Feel. Taste.*

I dreamt about you last night. You were on the corner of Hart Street, by the blue mural, and you smiled, but it was something not too funny. I came closer, and you backed away til you stood

at the mouth of an open garage, like the one on Main Street
in Flushing, 'cept there were giant red candy canes instead
of parking meters. And someone plucked one out and started
running. Police came — sirens, sirens. You had this look on your
face cuz the candy-cane stealer was your boy. And we ran, but
it was dark, and you went under some car and never came out.
I flew up the stairs till the sirens went away.

When I came down, I couldn't find you. And there were no
more cars in the parking lot.

*I had a dream too. I was watching BET on the couch with you in
my arms. Simple. Like rain.*

The COs call five minutes. I look up to breathe. See my girl
from Townsend Harris High at the corner table with a kid I
didn't know she had, patiently getting her forehead hiccied.
She straightens too, stretching a curved back. She sees me,
then decides she didn't. Guess it was gonna be like that. But
I understand.

*You know they count the weeks in here by Sundays?*
*Sunday Soul Trains.*

## Collector of Pigeon Feathers

We only speak when
he picks me up at
midnight to buy Marlboros
and tortilla chips
from the 7-Eleven
before driving home.

*I thought there would be more
than this,* he says. Revs
the MR2 engine, seats like
leather beds. We roar prone
though light-charred avenues.

He smacks a carton
on the flat of his hand.
My brother. GS —
Ghost Shadow.

My pool-hall, tucked-
trench-coat, cut-eyed wonder,
smoke writhed round
cheekbone. You stunned us
into seeing you.

Held a wedge of blade
against a driver's throat.
Sweat on sweat. Ran
with metal radio
hidden under wing.

They ran you down with
headlight and pistol
and handcuff.

You tried to make yourself
a man — your only offering, I know.

What rooms did we grow
apart in? Our father sleeps
in the bed, mother on the couch —
we all wanted more.

My forearm rests on the lip
of your window, hair whipped by I-95's
urgent air: another mystery we
ride, slipping in and out of light.

## Red

It is my sixteenth birthday. I spend it at Little's cousin Amalia's
apartment in Bushwick. Little spent the day cajoling his aunts
to bake me a pink Duncan Hines cake. Monica and Betsy dab
bits of frosting on with plastic white knives; Monica licks her
fingers. *Here*, she says. *Taste.* I lick them obediently: she is
still new to me. I smile, wanting her to like me. Two handfuls
of kids, all waist-size or smaller, mill around beneath us —
Keishla, Edel, Belsie, Desi, Shamika, JJ, Joey. I hold Angel at
my waist. He is sucking his sticky thumb.

Monica talks about the last abortion she had on Monday.
*My thirteenth one, ma. After Kayla I said no more. Fuck that.*
Thirteen? I mouthe to Little. He shrugs his shoulders as if to
say, *That's on her.* They gather round me in the living room and
sing happy birthday. We blow out candles over Frankie Ruiz
wailing *Vaya mi china!* from the back bedroom.

Amalia has a huge iron pot of rice and beans steaming on
the stove. *Take a plate before you go, mami.* She pushes me a
styrofoam plate wrapped in plastic, and I kiss the little kids
goodbye. Little has promised to take me to the top of the twin
towers for my birthday. I feel rushed and exhilarated when I
leave, a loud buzzing in my ears. *Take care of her*, Monica says
to Little. *It's a big thing, going into the city.*

*

When we reach the observatory, the sky has already begun to melt. A tissue-thin pink, like blood spilled in water. The city disappears underneath its haze, leaving only the quiet flicker of office lights. Little clenches my rose between his teeth. He hoists me on his back and runs me down the concrete strip. It is cool, and the wind lifts the hair from the nape of my neck.

Holding him above the sleeping city, under a sky that falls so red, so fast, the air crisp in my eyes, I tell him, I'm gonna remember this day forever.

*

On the way back to Flushing, we sit in the corner seats on the 7 train and make out, my legs slouched over his. An Asian straphanger spends his whole commute staring at me. He is my father's age, and glares at me with the same disgust my father would. It makes me stick my tongue down Little even further.

When I come home, my mother looks at my rose, my smeared mouth with a tired weight in her eyes. Turning around, she says, *Something happened to Jae. We going now.*

She refuses to answer my questions, so we ride silent in the Volvo to Jamaica. We get on the ramp to the Van Wyck Expressway. My mother's hands shake on the steering wheel.

*What you wear,* she spits, glancing at my red bodysuit. We try
to find parking outside the gates to Dara, the projects where
Jae and Gracie live, where we stayed with them when my mom
ran away from my dad. *Jae was attacked after school,* she says at
last. My head is in a whirl, hands wet. *Someone had to carry him
home.*

We don't need to open their door. It is unlocked, splayed open
to the dim-lit hallway. My aunt and Jae's mother stand around
him. We kick off our shoes and get closer. I can't see
his face for the women standing.

His white shirt is smeared with lashes of blood, and underneath
I see his ribs moving lightly. He lolls his head and looks at me,
forehead still brown from a boot print. Cauliflowers
of white stuff bubble around his left temple. One cheek torn
open. Later, he will have a scar like butterflies there. I try not
to wince. He looks at me, and I say softly, *Hey.*

*Nuna,* he says. *You didn't have to come.* Then, *Happy Birthday.*
*Jae,* I start. I am not crying, but water wells fast in my eyes.
*Someone go find his apa,* my aunt says. She ushers me into the
kitchen. *He left. Went crazy. He took a butcher knife, Issilah. He
went to kill them. Who? What? Who did it,* I demand. *Aiyu, I
don't know,* she says. *One black kid and one Spanish. Wearing
black hood and red vest.*

*So what if he kills them!* I spit. *They deserve it.* I feel as fragile as moth's wings ripped apart under the light. I want to stay with Jae, but the other women cradle him. *Go,* they say; none of them can drive. My aunt hands me her keys. My mother will take him to Jamaica Hospital, she says. And only I know Kissena Boulevard at night.

My aunt's Nissan has weak headlights. I look through the faint pools outside the window, at black gates, side alleys, parking lots, trying to find my uncle. Trying to find one black kid and one Dominican with a black shirt and red vest. For what? So I can kill them? Me — with my small, useless hands?

I think of my cousin, how he was walking home from Parson's Spring Concert. How they called him *chink, chink,* tried to rip off his Hilfiger jacket. Took his wallet and didn't believe he had less than two dollars. Turned his pockets inside out, kicked him beside a chainlink fence and turned him inside out. Stomped on his face. Other kids watched. Later Lisandro and Jonathan slung his limp body between them and carried him home.

I drive by National Wholesale Liquidators, the pizza shop, the Exxon, past the strangely quiet mouth of Pomonoc Housing. I think of my cousin, so stubborn he probably didn't say a word, just shook his head and wouldn't let go of his jacket, the only present he got last Christmas from his dad, who for once was still sober enough to remember.

A group of boys stand on the corner of P.S. 165. They are young, thin, and light-skinned, in t-shirts. Shoulderblades wing from their backs. One of them lights a blunt. They stare at me; I stare back as I roll by. One boy smiles, then puckers his lips.

They deserve to die, the black sweater, red vest. And then I remember that Little was wearing a red Polo sweater today, to match me. And I remember how I forgot to call him when I got home. How just before sunset, he carried me laughing on his back, a rose clenched in his teeth. How Monica baked a cake, and all the kids sang. And I am glad he is out in Bushwick and not in Jamaica tonight. And I hope my uncle remembers black sweater, red vest, not red sweater, black vest, and I drive in dark circles, hoping I won't find some blood that will make the ten o-clock news.

My crazed, drunk uncle with the sad-eyed smile, who never wanted to move into Jamaica. Because of black people who would steal in your face and call you names, knock over the rows of oranges you spent half an hour stacking. He didn't want to live crowded and ruffled against each other like pigeons. I stop in front of Parsons, park the car, walk around until I find him by the basketball hoops. Bent over the curb, sobbing.

I sit down next to him quietly and say *Samchun*. He looks at me, his face half-shadowed, saying *Ayu, Issulah, weh wassuh? Why are you here?*

*I don't know. . . I don't know . . . I love him*, I offer. He grabs my arm tightly, his knuckles like boulders. *Nadu*, he sobs. I have never seen my uncle's face like this. Something in my chest shifts. I've heard enough stories from my aunt about how he once slashed his own stomach open to show a would-be robber he was that crazy, to feel strong and helpless at the same time.

Now his eyes are not crazy, just broken. I want to put the knife back in them, to wash them over with bowls of warm water until they are new again. It is the same despair I feel with Little. But it is not my place to tell him such things, just to be there and hold the parts of him that are still intact.

I grab my uncle's hand, and we sit on the curb under the metal hoops. The knife lies by his feet, reflecting a line of gold from the streetlight.

## Sa-I-Gu

*"we are our first and last line of defense. me. you."*

~ k.w. lee

fire. if I touch
the screen my fingers
will singe or sing.

raw hands rip nikes
out of boxes, break glass
into white cobwebs.

my mother presses her hand
to her ruined lips.

*

we see grainy reels of a black fish
on concrete, arched,
kicked, nightsticked,

flopping, not fish but man —
here I rub my own tender
wrists, ask unanswerables —

*why are the cops doing this?*
my mother answers simply,
wisely, *because they are bad.*

of the looters, *because they are angry.*
and why hurt us — she chokes —
*because we are close enough.*

I sigh, slip under the fold
of her arm. she strokes my hair

and keeps me protected
as I must one day protect her.

\*

l.a.p.d. ring beverly hills like a moat,
won't answer rings from south central
furious and consistent as rain.

where did they hide, our women —
under what oil-stained
chevy did they breathe,

light, light, covering
the biting mouths
of wet-eyed children?

who pulled them
by hair into a riot
for a crime

they did not commit —

who watched and did nothing?

*

mile-high cameras hover,
zoom in, dub it
war of blacks & koreans,

watch us ripped
to red tendon for scraps
in a district, abandoned,

latasha shot on 50 channels,
not 200 shot korean grocers
whose names & deaths are kept local:

silence white as white silence.

we have no jesse
no martin no malcolm
no al, no eloquent, rapid tongue,

just fathers, thick-tongued,
and children too young to carry
more than straw broomstick and hefty bag.

all the women cry and hurl
what is not already shattered.

*

koreans mark disaster
with numbers.
4/29 — Sa-I-Gu.

south central — metal husks
of burnt cadillacs. exxon, michelin,
factories bare as cotton pockets.

this grocer with knotted tongue
stacks rows of bottles —
shining liquid copper.

he beats his son. no innocents here.
this customer slops in, slurs over
an Old E. no innocents here.

her hand hurls bottle and brick
for what is lost,
for what she cannot attain,
her open, laboring palm,
and the emptiness that
leans out to meet it.

his hand grips rifle on roof,
yes, for what is lost,
for what he, too, cannot attain,
his open, laboring palm,
his broken sign, burnt oranges.

god, it is a matter
of food to mouth,
of notions of *home* and *house*.

*

a son returns
with straw broomstick.

a daughter cooks rice
that steams untouched on the kitchen table,

slips off her mother's
devastated keds, slips her into bed.

two mornings after,
they march over ashes,

dust licking proud ankles.
30,000 koreans

sing in a language
most will never master:

[ *we shall overcome*
 *someday.*

**Sangmin,**

I imagined our babies too —
cut of eyelid, color of cheek

aigus, han, sarang
can stand untranslated.

\*

Our parents would arc
over us like tree branches sheltering

a roughly hewn road:
they would protect this one.

\*

Our mothers grew into women
in Daegu. They might have passed

the same river once
as girls, not knowing their children

would hold each other in the darkness
of another country as poem

and godbeauty and consolation.
Consolation.

## Maehyangri

The dirt road curls into a shoulder of rice paddy,
air hot against my face. The taxi driver jerks and stops
over loose gravel, hesitant to take us farther.
You students like danger, he hisses.

A mesh tent billows over red dust.
700 students sit in hunched waves, chanting songs
memorized years before I arrived.

Before us, a barbed wire wrapped with tissue
pink as blooming cosmos. Through its looped folds,
an expanse of green — outstretched lover, limbs supple —
Maehyangri: she lies breathless, sun a white disk

in the indifferent sky. I snap pictures of do-or-die
students handkerchiefed against tear gas,
dressed to go to Orchard Beach more than a rally . . .

A woman strays in front of the barbed fence,
baby strapped with a blanket to her bent back;
to our left, a farmer poking police an arm's length
away from her trodden crops.

And the students are rioting. Young cops brandish
sapling sticks. Hot with confusion, we swing at each other,
each crack stippling my ears. We swing at each other:

young Korean brother of split cheekbone
and torn shirt, young Korean sister,
fingers ripped by scissored wire. We are killing each other
again. *Helenah, hold my hand —*

a young man stumbles out, eyes feral. I hold him up gently,
blood seeping through my fingers, soothe him with banmal:
*yah, illu wah, genchanah.* We inhabit a quilted space,
a cupped moment of healing. And I realize:

what I want is time for her torn hands, his split
wood-carved cheek, to heal; for respite for this bruised,
beautiful valley, for the marrow of my people tainted with pollution
and shaking from vibrations of dropped US bombs;

for babies with cotton-stuffed ears,
for boys who dream to the drone of 747s —
I want a silence so clean it baptizes.

## Canasí

~ for Llane

By the mouth of a river
that dreams of being a sea,
I pick up a shock of flamboyán
and wreathe you in red petals.

You sing Brazilian acapella
armed with 40 pieces of bread
rationed in blue plastic bags. We walk

to escape La Habana, who bathed us
in bus fumes, police who arrested you
for kissing a man in Coppelia park,
to shed my skin from hisses of *china, china* . . .

At dawn, our skin tight
and scarlet as cold plums
from sleeping in an outdoor train station,
the sky, a ruptured storm blessing.

I'm with you,
my face is burning.
How can you look at me
as if I were a sunset, a sea, a mirror?

You say an island is not just an island
and a country is as complicated
as its smallest sick child.

Today vultures circled;
we were trailed by hens,
dogs, memories.

Today love was the thin blue blanket
cloaking us on a truck ride,

a honey soda drink
that cost 2 pesos,

the pregnant stray dog
that accidentally bit my fingers
for meat, for sheer hunger,

your cloth turban and pink eyeshadow . . .
even two soldiers
demanding ID —

love, that long bus home
that could have been a disco.

*¿Es verdad que las esperanzas deben regarse*
*con rocío?*
Is it true our desires must be watered
with dew?

— Pablo Neruda

## The Temperature of This Water

You left an hour ago,
trudging down the dirty slush road
with a flippant wave of scarf

*have fun in L.A.*
*have fun in Samaritan House.*

And although I know the shower will get cold
as I write this, I want to record what is true,
the glimpses of you around my apartment
that unravel me:

the green lighter on the lip of the bathroom sink,
green plaintains yet unmashed,
half-cooked rice and beans damp in a pot —
you thought you could stop
and return to it later —
my sweaters drying on a rack, lit by the window,
the Big R supermarket receipt
crumpled on the corner of the table,
chicken cutlet, .13 lb. @ 1.49 lb.,
dark skirts
hung over every wooden chair
like veils of mourning,
the refuse of laundry
strewn out on our futon,
unmanageable as my hair,

the temperature of this water,
as if you're coming back.

## Portrait of a Bronx Bedroom

carnival mask
     bedsheet tacked over window
          ice freezing on silver bumpers
               lime-green el train rolling away
               dazed windows

copper Bronx cockroaches
     corroding the sink

light hitting soft skin above my chest,
     silence to pool in, plum-red congas

                    what sexy music
              wine and whiskey arguments
       what thrown dishrag
         dirty boot,

     which room needs
         a match lit
         hiss of warm light

5 blanket broken heater
winter dizzy with cold
        whose mouth, whose
           soft eyelids and long limbs

      secrets we covet behind doors shut  tight as lips
        how will my bones succumb to blackness?

what dumb picture will outlast me?

all this sitcom, dirty couch, just a moment

who will continue to love me?
                                          who will I die loving?

Let's take this night
        over graves
            let's illuminate
                this cupped space,
                    your mouth

                        a hot black flower

## Little

The first time I met Little, I kissed him. At night, in the middle of a four-lane highway, on one of those concrete strips wide enough for just you and a frail row of young maples, trunks held up by green spirals. It was a kiss I wanted and a kiss he gave, a kiss that made Karina's mother watch me with steady dark eyes before she released the lace curtain and stood, shadowed and small, against the apartment's screen door.

Since then, it's always been like this: a kiss, a disapproving stare. Little's hair twisted and frolicked on his head, wrapped in green, red, yellow, blue rubberbands, the cuff of his jeans rolled up on his left leg. His back housed a skeleton jester rolling a pair of wild dice. A small scar interrupted the perfect bow of his upper lip. In other words, he was beautiful. Dangerous. Even more so because of his shy lisp, eyes framed with incredible lashes, broken words falling over each other in handwritten love notes that I kept stashed on my bookcase in a plastic bag wrapped with red Godiva ribbon stolen from work.

It was like this. In the morning, I'd get to school late, then would be 15 minutes later because I'd stop to tell Leroy the security guard details of my night with Little. I wrote his nickname on the yellow dividers in my binder and continued my Little saga during third period. David and Bret, two Jewish boys who sat behind me, were obsessively interested in my sexual progress reports. During lunch, I shared anecdotes with my group of seven girlfriends. We dubbed '93 the year of fuckfest because so many of us lost our virginity in record numbers.

In between was just filler. PSAT vocabulary words, declining the word "girl" in Latin (puella, puellae, puellae, puellam, puella), algebraic equations whose answers split into halves and led into random sets or infinity. Learning perspective in Mr. Morales' art class by drawing a dot in the center of a line that roads, fences, and trees would lean into before disappearing altogether.

What did it matter? All lessons led back to Little. I closed my eyes in my heart of minds and imagined us, the one night we spent together, the slight weight of his hands and dry expanse of his palms, his curls holding dewlike drops of water in the shower, his thin stalks of legs and astonishingly hairy buttocks. His malformed big toe with its tiny yellow chip, more of a mistake than a toenail. His wide, muscular back rippling over me, the v-shaped bowl of his hipbones that my hands loved to hold in the dark.

This matters, I would tell myself. More than the four nights I spent waiting for his call, interrupting the natural order of my house to rush, pick-up, and check for the payphone buzz. More than the time he looked at the hair I spent an hour curling and said, *What the fuck is that.* More even than the time I stood waiting outside school one October afternoon after six buses had taken all the kids away, and I watched the dead leaves whorl on the street, feeling in them the sinking motion of my stomach. I'd ended up taking the Q25/34 alone, pretending I'd come home late from watching Kuem-Hee play volleyball.

To conjugate "girl" meant wondering how many girls and types of girls he had been with. To memorize difficult vocabulary words meant a pang in my chest at all the beautiful words he'd never get to learn; to see math problems grow more difficult and possess multiple answers thrilled my chest to the uncertainty of life; to the uncertainty and multiple directions our relationship could go depending on who saved whose life.

## Dangerous Boys, Dangerous Men

You can be owned by Love. By Fear. By Duty. By the Past. Cycles in the solar system and social system whose orbits were predetermined and set centuries before your birth, aligned again after your death. Cycles of Bottles. Firewater. Pipes. Perfumed Breath.

February on Linden Street. Still cold enough to see the echoes of your breath, but the slim trees had just begun to thaw, ice melting off the tips of black front gates. I sat in Little's cracked green studio, in front of a disheveled wooden drawer that hung open like a slack mouth, a fistful of phone numbers wrinkled in my hand.

He shoved me on the bed and locked me inside with strewn numbers on torn matchbooks, my hair like rags, a stashed bottle of Palo Viejo.

I drank myself raw, fire scorching my throat until it turned into smooth water. I propped open the paint-chipped window, stood on its ledge, debating flight. Swaying to the stares of passing men.

The world left me behind, he'd left me behind, a green humming mess, and when the world returned, when he unlocked the door and entered, he found me drenched in sweat, rocking in front of a cracked mirror, laughing and crying and singing to my own wet reflection.

And I started to talk about his mother, who had died that fall from AIDS. *Remember that Christmas we were all together, opening presents in the stocking? The Lollipops? The sweaters. She liked my gifts. I miss it. I miss it. You never talk about her. Why? Why?* He sat flint still. I blabbered until I realized his mouth

was moving, words I could not hear — *shut up, shut up* — it
escalated, and he slammed me against the bureau. *Shut up!*

I slapped him. He slapped me back. It hummed in my ears. I
had one chance to look him in the eyes before he punched me
in the stomach. I fell to my knees as he kicked me, kicked me
out the door, down the stairs, punched my hands off the grip
of the railing. Into a livery cab.

That should have ended it. Click of the door, curling in bed.
Standing undressed and awed at the bruised green map of
my body. But it wasn't. Because we love to punish others and
punish ourselves by pushing things over the inevitable edge.
Is it flight? Or falling? Maybe falling reckless is the closest we
thought we could get to flight.

Which finds me, three years later, on Tower Air with him to
Aibonito. Which finds me, five years later, flinging a rollerblade
at his head in Flushing Meadow Park. Which finds us both tired
and tattooed with scars, trying to forgive and love and forget.

## House of Sharing
Comfort Women

*I can forget everything when I sing,*
*when the blood is burnt up.*

Drunk from pots filled
with rice wine, she pulled a quilt
over her mouth to cover her smell,
listened to Nam Insoo through the blanket,
stack of song books
piled by the foot of her yoh.

*I was 14.*

Flash flood melts the road into a river.

*3 pine trees. My parents thought*
*they sent me to a good place.*
*My hands like rubber gloves.*
*My heart bleeding.*

This halmoni, silver-streaked hair
marcelled down her neck,
in a hanbok of 5 layers like
a white lotus.

She wipes red-pepper stains
from the concrete windowsill, thin
tissue shredding in her fingers.

At the sill, she tells me to keep secrets
from my man, even if he is good. *No one
should open all your contents. You don't
even know the word for contents?* She sucks her teeth
and closes the window.

They cut her open
because she was too small.
With rusted scissors. Virgin. Doctor
first to enter her after the operation.

She ate rice balls prone on stone bed,
thin mattress, one washcloth to rinse
between soldiers. Beheaded
if she bit down.

*I can forget everything when I paint,
when the blood is burnt up.*

I cannot reconcile this halmoni
with a girl 50 years ago,
lips like a folded heart, neck
long as reed, who never learned to write
her own name, this halmoni, bundled thick
in two wool coats, bus ticket to her 882nd rally
clenched tightly in gloved fist, pushing
glass-shielded policemen
young enough to be grandsons
to be in spitting distance
of the Japanese embassy.

She draws a painting
larger than herself of a soldier
in mustard green, wrapped to a cherry blossom tree
with black barbed wire, guns pointed
at his chest from 3 directions, white doves
taking flight from its branches,
white doves taking flight, and she danced like this,

hands flicking, hip jutting,
wrinkles filling her eyes,
ash falling from her cigarette,
cup of macculi splashing, upraised,
she danced like this.

## The Street That Curves Into Itself

In Aibonito,
eating homemade piñas from plastic cups,

Estelita laughed at my metal spoon scrapings. She told me,
*This is how you eat an icie. With your tongue.*

*Suck it, soften it. It'll come out.*
*Turn it around and eat the sweet side.*

*This is how we do it here.*

\*       \*       \*

. . . this is how we do it here?

My mother asked Freddy, *Don't you feel bad cheating on your wife all*
    *the time?*
He said, *Don't you get tired of eating the same thing all the time?*

Here we are, stained in yellow, tiny as cockroaches,
eyes violent and exposed to the world.

I study this picture to see how my face belies loss,
what quiet song when nobody listens:

a hum.
Waiting brutal there, in the night —

\*       \*       \*

A street in Aibonita curves into itself.
You call it la manzana, Estelita, el corazón.

## Because #12

the carpet is dirt flecked and mauve
you are intensely watching *Moesha* while I write this
it is November
our radiator is as cold and dead as a museum installation
you haven't sucked me dry in two months

I used to watch your eyelids soft in sleep
and think you were the most beautiful person to grace my bed
I still do

we have long and protracted train arguments about spilled lotion
when I ask you well? say something
you say I love you as a defense mechanism

*

I yell at you in front of strangers on the L train

you stumble into our apartment with fingertips trembling
from the dime bag of perico
you think I don't know you inhaled

I have already cried too many nights without you

they say my uterus is scarred with pink, leaflike veins

my heart feels like a cliff people dive off of

*

my lover plants trees in wrong seasons
so crisp, diamond leaves freeze on stems

*

I have craved guava and lemon juice and beef marrow
and you do not know how it feels
I have dry heaved, wet-eyed, throat raw, in front of Chinese
restaurants
and you cannot know how it feels

grown up in a house where plates struck walls more often than laughter

like all other Christian, Mormon, Islamic, Catholic, born-again
self-righteous hip-hop men
who will never hold a life at your very center
and decide which way it will pass
between your legs

you do not understand that regardless what form
something will spill

thighs, breasts, heart will never forget

my womb is not a billboard designed to carry out your beliefs

I still cry at night wrapped up like the fetus inside me

remember showers that dropped me into vertigo
wet thunder of two heartbeats

*

you are my lost sky and salt

you are my lost sky and salt

anemone in the breeze

*

I am selfish

this is the only self I have to love

*

it is November
our radiator, cold and dead as a museum installation

we argue about spilled lotion

I have watched your eyelids soft in sleep and have loved you
I still do

## Miracle

Once, a father who sold fish
discovered his son
was a Flushing gangster
who extorted restaurants,
robbed livery cabs
at knifepoint, and bought
cigarettes and pizza
for older gangsters.
Sobbing, he beat his son
for the first time,
each thud throbbing
like the long-dead planks
trembling under his boots.

The son ran away, slept
in pool halls
on burnt, uncovered
mattresses, had sex
with a prostitute,
felt aloneness
wrap around him
like a wool blanket.

He returned at Christmas
to help with the fish store
filled with hungry,
ticket-waving Italians.

He cashiered alone,
dozed in the heated Nissan,
smoked Marlboros,
wept only once.

His father watched him,
wanting to tear the blond
streaks out of his hair.
They moved in silence
through the freezer-cold stretches
of pre-Christmas Eve,
packing orders, tying blue bags,
hauling them onto shelves,
ordering *more salmon, more halibut,*
*more cocktail shrimp.*

The son, apron dirtied
and smelling like socks,
sat on top of a white freezer box,
his worn boots
hanging over the side.
He leaned into his fists,
cap over his eyes.

His father took a whisk
from a blue inhaler,
then knelt
on the black tile's
gleam and kneaded
his only son's legs,

from ankle to knee,
slowly, slowly, through
the battered jeans.

Under the pale pool
of fluorescent light,
one bulb broken,
two dim, the son let him,
the son let him.

## Zola Kai Mabel Hisae Chiati Cindy Feliz

Girl. There is nothing small about you.
Late nights tangled in phonecord, rubbing our forearms against January,
rubbing our asses against bulging khakis at Nell's.

We stand in front of smoky bathroom mirrors, paint under-eye hollows,
ready battle face to take men down with a sidelong glance.

You are my girl, Mabel. As I lie in this apartment, bent over by the
       wind of a trifling man, your voice wraps me in blankets,
helps me grow like I grew out of shoulder-grazing, gold-plated hoops
and attitude to match, all that fake stuff I put on.

You are my girl, Hisae, straddling men in thin-walled rooms,
overhearing each other's love sighs, going on joyrides in stationwagon
from Negril to MoBay. We hit Copa, the Quarter,
stumbled through Eddie Torres together,
soaped each others' gold, round bodies and slept like it wasn't a thang.

Those were the days, Cindy. Big-lipped, kaboom booty,
snapping-Wrigleys. Chinese woman. Your insecurities
& latest *Stress* magazine tucked safe into the Prada.
You were me, magnified.

We both dating motherless men (our parents
refused to shake their outstretched hands),
men who took our money, loved us with sheet-gripping,
whirlwind passion, girlfriends' advice scattered like
uprooted houses. We eye to I in the center of the storm.

You died last week. 80 miles per hour.
He killed you. Sunday car accident.

Y'all were probably arguing just like I was,
2:30 in the morning, with a man who simultaneously
fills and drains your heart,
a cracked pitcher.

Flashback to the brake-screeching nights I've had with Little,
how many times death seemed just short of impossibility
and life, a mere backdrop to our fists slammed on dashboard.

Girl, we be the iron tracks hammered into unforgiving ground,
riding parallel into destruction. What happened? You gone
and I'm left standing in the ragweed, broke Heinekins, and charred pebbles.

Zola sobs, *you need to be careful, Ishle. Please.*
Wish whispers of *love you. Call me when you get home.*
*Girl. He don't know what he got.* Or, *you your best thing.*
Womangirl. Gather your split peach, sad honey, ice-pick self —
gather your beauties and believe in them.

Zola Kai Mabel Hisae Chiati Cindy Feliz
We be broken spirit housed in scarred body, not all strong sistas, not
        all queens;
we haunt disco/club/poetry/house/street, try to step into our skin
        and cherish it.
Under mute heaven and streetlight — I have to love you, girl,
        becuz you me,
and we're stepping into this journey together.

## Lions

He sleeps until 4:30 then carefully gells his hair
while she watches the sun slide down an old brownstone

the way her mouth ran down another man's neck.
He pays for her Nikes rocking bundles

on the corner of Hart and Wilson.
She wants to be his mother,

lover, and sister again,
but this time, do it right;

dreams of ripping scars
into the faces of women she has never met.

He barfs out the window;
she tells jokes nobody laughs at —

lights on the river flicker orange —

he wants her
to save him.

She wants a trial without his lawyer
massaging her shoulders on the E train.

She swallows him to keep him from leaving,
nibbles at his fingertips, kneecaps,

ankles, wrists, until she reaches
bone marrow and starts the tender sucking.

There is a line, an arc, and a rip.
He is startled awake at the red doors opening;

everything is passing her by
backwards.

A fluorescent smear across
avenues and dark apartments.

He flips through photos of her, legs spread,
holding his curly head down to her crotch:

she's standing on a flowered twin bed,
reflected in the mirror, he thinks, like a goddess.

He marches into the mouths of lions
with a wry smile.

She remembered that she had once drank
from this well.
She remembered that she had walked very
far.

— Theresa Hak Kyung Cha

## Korean Lullaby

1.

Last night, three words
from our Korean lullaby
entered my dream:
*Du man gang* . . .

Our old picture still exists,
buried in the silver suitcase:
you pregnant, me shy. I like us
frozen in those awkward, real stances.

We drive across state lines in silence
to avoid sitting at a dinner table
where any minute laughter can
spill in your face
like an overturned glass, upset
by a man who shares your bed
but not your language.

We were never young together,
and *daughter* is not how you see me
after three long drags in a clean kitchen,
two hours after we redden our knees
picking up slivers of clear glass
that sparkled linoleum like sunlit snow.

Arizona,
highland desert plains,
crocodile-cracked earth maze.

Driving across state lines,
twice, in silence,
the horizon trapped under
our windshield, car seats
smelling of Kent 100's,
burnt matches.

## 2.

There is a burning in the air
and she wonders where her mother is.

Edel saw Tootie glut another kid on Knickerbocker,
the sweet sound of curses up our route.
We halt and glaze.

A touch of hands —
what signifies lovers, friends,
drug dealers.

We're counting nights
unseen under boardwalks, in pool halls,
daring to die in August's riffs.

This flyaway night so weak, rubber-felt . . .

**3.**

I would like to remain like this always,

inhabiting quiet pools between music,
the acoustics of an empty heart.

I see this in Johemil's mouth
biting her baby Louie on the ass
as he crawls over the bunk bed,
laughter pealing through their dark apartment.

**4.**

*It is not a coincidence that our mother died when we were young,*
*and none of us knows how to sing.*
                    — Suja

Crevice of water where you almost drowned,
the look on your face when you realized
I couldn't save you.

Beyond fairy pools and leper islands and silver dime-store turtles,

home.
Marked more by songs and shoelaces
than flags, songs folded.
Lullabies.

Just three words, the rest I cannot remember,
and you are not here to give them to me.

## Apa

One word about my father — he wanted to live. And he didn't
mind killing. He knew silence, the way the woods breathe.
How to quiet his youngboy skin enough to ease into a pond,
snatch and skin frogs, and sell them to local farmers as chicken
feed. Ten frogs for a handful of sugar balls. Exhilarating — the
catch, the kill, the candy.

Maybe that's what drew my mother to him: he was a wild one.
A runt, with short, spiked hair, and thighs that were slowly
hardening into boulders. Back then, he could do anything.
Ram into startled chests yelling *yah! jashiga*, while scrambling
around a tackle. Catch a torn leather rugby ball thrown
between two grown men or fly weightless though the air. Tour
with the Seoul national team; compete in China, Japan, Korea.

My dad and his teammates sang hoarsely in Seoul University's
bar after a victory, way before karaoke, the whole room joining
the chorus. Way before stripping fish calloused his hands and
his dreams. Way before me. Through the drunk ruckus, dim
lights, the flicker of soju through shot glasses on the table, she
saw him. His bright teeth, finely cut cheekbones, gold eyes.
He saw her lit cigarette, unruly hair, her wry, wide smile.

This is the way I imagine it on nights when I am forgiving.
I know there must have been some wick lit, some smoke and

burn, although neither of them will admit or pain themselves to remember. I cling to this because I know she drank, she smoked, she was wire-thin, sarcastic, stunning. He wanted it. Her rock-climbing hands. Her quick mind and quicker mouth, so unlike the mute, wide-eyed girls trailing him from game to game. He sensed that she was a survivor, alone. So he bumped his way next to her at the bar and started their marriage with a joke.

## Kunemo

Don't marry man full of joke! I told your mother. Did she
listen? Anyway, who listens in your family? So now she stuck.
Aiyu. Stubborn heads. Like you. Like a peanut.

I was so upset she got married. In that ugulee dress. Make her
look sick! I made her a beautiful gown for wedding — yes. I
sewed it. With pattern. Off white, simple, A-line. Elegant. And
your grandmother threw it away. Too plain, they said. Too
simple. See? They have no taste. Look at this picture. No taste.

So I stayed in America. Why? I had to work. Edmond, my
husband, was going crazy. Oh, he grew a beard and wore old
clothes. Drank so much, took drugs with his beatnik friends.
Not hippy — beatnik. The cool ones. But he looked complete
like a crazy! Like a caveman. Even my neighbor, this old man,
American, said to me once, *Is that your husband? I feel bad
for you.* Even he said this to me, a Korean!

Oh, I was so depressed, Issilah. I thought I was gonna die. I
was sick, physically sick. Stuck in bed. Weak.

You know who saved me? Suk Soon — Mrs. Maycomb. Yes.
She helped me a lot — imagine, two poor Korean girls in
Connecticut. Aigu. She had garden in her backyard, by the
corn, with all kinds of flowers. Not food garden — tulips, roses,

cosmos, daisy. So I helped her dig. Every morning, 6 am. My
hands, the dirt. It worked.

I went to library. Took out books on compost, needlework.
Patternmaking. And I taught myself how to garden and cook
and sew, reading books. I was 29. Step by step. My English not
even so good. It was hard. But I did it. Step by step — if you
do like that, you can do anything.

So I grew my own garden. In back of our shed house. I
even grow some of those marijuana once! Oh, I don't know.
Edmond's friends threw it back there, I didn't know what it
was. But it was pretty, so I watered it. And it grew fast. Up
to my shoulders like that.

Did I ever smoke? No. Just once. It gives me headache. Don't
do it. It makes you dumb.

But Edmond smoke all the time. Aiyu, I couldn't stand it. I
always went into bedroom when they came. All this friends.
Thought he was a brilliant. Even one professor said it — he is
genius. So I think he was smart, in the beginning, but then the
drugs, and his brain — it runs in his family — he lost his mind.

One day I come home and no furniture. No nothing. He just
threw out everything and said, we don't need it. We're moving
to Mexico. My clothes, forks, spoons, my china plate collection.

He dumped it. Terrible, terrible. Things like that all the time. Did we go? No, no. We drove to Nova Scotia instead. In a borrowed car. We were lucky. It was the '60s. We stayed with an old couple who liked our face.

But even his mother, on dying bed, said to me, *You better get out while you still can. Get out! He will ruin you.* His own mother!

So I divorced him. Even that he wouldn't give me. He write long letters to other women at the table, make phone calls, and still he won't give me divorce. Aigu, Issilah. Ten years with that man. He almost killed me! I mean it. So you, you have to find a good one, easy. You don't need that. Don't go through it. So be . . . careful. Okay, Issilah? Be smart. Or don't marry at all. Who cares? You don't need husband. For what? But don't tell your mother I said that.

## Uma

My mother was the biggest love of my life. Before I could
speak English, I'd curl into the pleats of her khakis. I'd hang up
phones so people wouldn't wake her. I wedged my body
between her and the pillow when my father once tried to
smother her. All my early intelligence, I think, was born of the
intense desire to please her. I held in my piss. Stopped wearing
diapers. Twitched a shoulder-raising dance to make her laugh
instead of scratching off my chicken pox.

After my father beat her and retreated to the hot silence of his
room, filled with the fuzz and glare of tv, I would sit near her
in the soft corners. But not too close, I learned. Such times
she'd flinch from my touch.

I knew her responsibilities intimately: to cook, to clean, to
stay home, scrub tub, set table, make dinner, stay home, stay
home, stay home. Once I sat through a children's play about
leprechauns with an audience full of other kids, my stomach
tight with fear because it was 5:30 and cutting close to dinner.
The green felt costumes with sharp, pointed edges, the painted
faces and frenetic children running on stage dizzied and
terrified me. *What time is it? Let's go. Let's go home.*

Another afternoon: fallen leaves and a series of wooden
balancing beams stacked higher and higher around a rusted

playground in Bayside. I balanced on them, fingers latched lightly in my mother's hand until, high above her head, I let go and ran. She'd let me run reckless.

She possessed that serrated, metal tinge that bared its edges when he wore her down. His endless hisses and epithets — *shangnyunah, shibhalnyun!* — left us lying on our sides like dull knives. Then she'd bark something harsh and exacting, about his mother being a dog. His face would startle awake, a streak of hurt and shock flashing across his cheeks before he pummeled into her. A rush of bile and water filled my belly. For her.

Funny, he'd never hit us, just lift and carry us by our pajamas, gently, to the next room. Hit me, I'd cry. Hit *me*. My father would look at me with disgust and surprise before shaking his head and locking the door.

## A Simple Bridge

These days I feel out of touch with lightning,
fire, even the loneliness of wind.

My soul sings to itself
because it is alone.

And then, I think lightning,
fire, wind are all solitary forces:

they can't help but touch
things in their path. It is the reaching —

the space between the paper's edge,
the blue fingers of flame,

between the wind
and sharp, breathless leaves,

between the whiteblue jolt,
the one bare tree,

branches open to light
and burning —

it is a simultaneous distance
and longing my body recognizes.

A simple bridge inside me
waits to be crossed by lovers

in both directions — who meet
in the middle of the arc at four hours:

the pink hour, the pitch hour,
the starless hour, the soft, waking hour.

## Pool and Poetry
~ for the CAAAV Sisters

We roll deep down Fordham with a baby carriage
to Mr. Lee's pool hall. Kim, Rothny, and Rothana
grace tables with the cool of black ravens.
Kim aims and shoots,

fingers arched over poolcloth
with mathematical precision,
slow click of the cue ball against the nine
that rolls to its pocket
smooth and easy as fate.

*It's a bet. Teach me pool and I'll teach you
poetry.* In St. Mary's convent
we write quotes on our graffiti blackboard
like *an eye for an eye leaves the world blind*
and *God grant me the serenity . . .*

Through a stained-glass Jesus,
D cops an ounce of Jekyll &
Hyde off young dealers on Briggs.
Rothana daily navigates sidewalks of left dog shit
and crumpled Wise bags.

Kim throws Rothny a handball across the pool room
right above the baby's curled forehead, and Rothny
catches it with swift, thoughtless precision.

From this, I know they hurl themselves in the air
like hawks — dip, swoop, fling, and soar.
They know how magic sings in their limbs
and how to play Bainsbridge at twilight —
girls standing in position, ready to leap
into the women they want to become.

**Uma in Pieces**

I.

In my dream, my mother is flying again,
and besides bumping into the streetlight
in the sharp ascent, she makes her way fast
to the other side of town, but then
the red parachute slips off her shoulders
and she falls . . . and I see her,
falling so long, it seems, falling so slowly,
I am able to run to the place
she landed and be there
moments after she fell . . .
*I felt I was falling so long*, she said.
*You were*, I said, and thought it my fault
for not tying the strings right.
My mother lay there, still and stiff like the days of my childhood
when she was always bedridden and flat on the mattressed floor,
towel on her head, eyes closed. Once again
a mother I could not help. I stepped away,
I stepped away, leaving her unprepared, thinking only later
how I failed to ask if anything was broken,
if all her parts were moving,
staying only to touch her hands for a brief while,
not massaging them.

II.

Looking back now,
I see her two hands
hidden in a mass of curly hair,
lighting and smoking Kent 100's,
thumbing through Korean want ads,
twirling the extra-long
phone cord, handling dishes
a little too loudly for dinner.

How I saw her leaning against the wall, one leg up,
newspapers spread in a disorganized fan around her.
Saying timidly, you can do it ma,
and she threw one at me — it fluttered in my face
like the wing of a crazed bird — and she screamed,
*Leave me alone, no I can't.* Yes you can, I stuttered.
*No I can't*, she said, I think she was crying,
the hot light in her eyes
cutting my face into shreds.

III.
We ate pizza in the Cross County parking lot,
and I did not question it. My mom sometimes has these cravings,
a slice of pizza, a bagel, a bowl of jja jang myun.
Between bites, I heard about a phone he threw.
*Luckily I ducked,* she said, *but what if I didn't . . .*
I nod, and she continues as if we were talking about the weather,
or an overheard conversation.

We talk through the sides of our mouths,
vision always fixed on a platform pole, a streetlight,
a newsstand, a skateboarder receding into the distance.

IV.

*I passed the telephone interview yesterday,* she says.
I think, oh, that's what it was.
I was scared to go into the living room
when she was pressing the phone buttons
all afternoon; thought she had gone a bit crazy.
You know how crazy people do repetitive things
to calm themselves into gentle psychosis . . .
*They have benefits,* I hear, *Northwestern, Pacific, Medicare, health aid,*
*travel discounts, frequent flyers.*
Through this cloud I hear her oh nyah Daegu laughter,
smell her cold fish and freezer air. Through this cloud,
I feel her warm hands against my stomach, healing
my menstrual cramps, and every atom of my body
stills for the moment in my mind when her bent back
straightens off the mattressed floor,
her hand wipes the curls from her face,
her eyes rise, and she says, *Things are different now* . . .
When I come back, she is asking me,
sitting on the corner of my cramped twin bed,
*Should I take it?* and I think of how much I love her,
how she is my heart and my uma and the reason I am alive,
how I am caught by her stunning, watchful eyes —
those eyes that have been missing my eyes
for too long, and I say, *God, Uma.*
*Take it, Take it.*
*Take it.*

## Queen Min Bi

Queen Min was the bomb. Smooth forehead, perfectly
parted thick hair and plum lips at fourteen,
enough to make any pedophile happy.
So the king handpicked her,

orphan Korean girl born in Yuhju,
to be a royal marionette — no one guessed
she owned a wooden heart to match any politician's.
Maybe she abused her handservants.

Maybe she pumped into her husband doggy style
with an early Korean bamboo strap-on,
and that's why she never had children.
Maybe that made Hwang so happy, even after she died,

throat sliced open by invading Japanese,
he hand-carved her name into a slab of man-sized marble,
honoring a woman who snatched his kingdom
without a glance back at history,

what those scrolls dictated for female behavior.
I want to be like her, befriending pale-skinned foreigners,
infuriating her father-in-law enough
for him to conspire towards her death
while commoners rested head to stone pillow

and dreamt of her brow-raising power;
16 when she married, 32 when she died —
before Japanese flags cloaked our country,
before Korean housewives lay beaten

without laws to halfway shield
their swollen faces. Half a world away,
yisei Korean children flinch at the smack of skin
on skin, memorize the hiss of curses like bullets,

and I wish she were more than dust and legend, a sold-out opera
at Lincoln Center or part of a wistful poem;
I want to inherit the tiger part of her, the part that had me
tracing the clay walls of her birthplace

with my fingers in the rain, wanting
to construct a woman out of myth.
So by Chinese calendar, she's a rabbit, her favorite
drink was macculi, Korea's homemade moonshine,

her left breast slightly heavier than her right,
and maybe she kissed her husband on the forehead
before overtaking his kingdom as Queen Min Bi,
so loved by all they called her Mama.

## Rosaries

When I get a night to think beyond the crowded rooms
of my life and remember what out there makes me write,
my throat catches fire to realize Johemil is still suckling her baby
and adjusting Louie's small cap, carrying her whole carriage
down the L train. Anna Li Sian lays breathless over the heat
skimming her chest while a thousand seagulls are flying —
Raspberry is braiding China's hair, and the fall of light
against the back of the East River must be breathtaking,
and sunsets will break over Bushwick, Southside, and Oakland,
and starfruit contain the shape of a star inside them,
and Mariposa stands inside a Nuyorican strobelight, cursing, singing,
and crying, and Benji's mother is out there, trying her best to raise
a girl that isn't hers while Betty is trying to do her best
with one that is, because Kunemo is cooking galbi and kimchee
bibim bab, and Ed Garcia is skydiving while Pilate grips her husband
falling through the air, because Taiyo is rhyming on the corner
of Linden and Cypress, David Blaine is levitating, and Sze Pui
is writing on a fire escape, because Little will hold my mouth
in his mouth, because Sangmin is holding his mother, crying,
because there is rocking, because there is motion,
because there is light.

## Railroad

One day I will write a poem
about my father as a mountain,
and there will be no shame for the dynamite
and the blasted hole, the pickaxes and steam drills
paving their own resolute path,
for the railroad ploughed through his core,
for shattered rocks, for pungent scent of pines.
My father will be a mountain surrounded by wind
that wears him down as slowly as marriage,
as America, as time. But he is still
a man and a mountain: drilled, hammered, alive,
unaware of all who love him from the far track.

## Culebra Revisited

I.

San Juan, Huracao. *Stop it, please!*
Ishmael is dying. *Let him sleep.*

II.

Here, more like lovers than family,
we halt more than talk
and your sisters ache for
Brooklyn.

Drowning is a soft, private thing. I feel it most
in this place without water.

III.

When very dusk, Nelson sits by the deck
waiting for his mother
to blow into shore.
*(Everywhere I go, I carry me with me . . . )*

Chavo scratches his neck
with a plastic fork

We search for clams,
flashlights in green water.

*Next time, they tell me, use Tower Air,
and remember to take two blankets each
from the plane.*

What I remember most are the light
of candles in brown paper bags,

the light in your eyes when
exposed to water.

*(sun dying)*

*This coral,* you say. It's the exact shape
of a woman bending over backwards.

I am so glad you see.

**Steven Outside the Fish Store**
(December 1998)

Tired of hauling 40 pound bags of seafood back to the freezer,
Steven rubbed his red, grooved palms and pushed out doors,
sat on the curb and smoked a Marlboro. Our sweaters stank of
sweat and cold fish, his feet so swollen he ditched the sneakers
and wrapped his feet in plastic bags with twist-tie strings tied
up around his ankles. He talked, and snow fell around us like
dust motes, then flakes full as baby's fists, blanketing the park-
ing squares and wetting our pink, flushed faces. I looked at him
sideways, this cousin of mine who relatives called thin and
reclusive, remembered feeding him with a bottle, weekend
sleepovers whispering over the bodies of limp, drunk fathers,
this kid with slim, elegant fingers who invented whole books
for book reports before he got his head kicked in by a black kid
and a Dominican hissing *chink, chink,* and he looked so beauti-
ful this night, through snow, his shallow breaths haloing the air,
laughing and rubbing his frostbitten feet, and I wanted to
freeze him right there, keep things as clear and crisp as they
appeared this Christmas Eve: a throat-burning shot of my baby
cousin Steve, rubbing his raw hands and smoking.

## Ode to the Picnic Singers, 1984

. . . And then at dusk the mother
climbed atop the picnic table
and belted out a Patty Kim hit,
plastic spoon a clutched mic in her fist,

and the galbi spit and bubbled
dark as azalia and crushed black diamond,
meat soy-sauced and sizzling in the July heatwaves
that hummed like the yellow frisbee flung

over tiny Youna Ean, kneeling among clover and dandelion.
Aigu, the sky flapped above us like a soiled workshirt on a clothesline
while we twisted our ankles over Chinese jump rope,
then flew by on flowered banana seats, wind teasing the streamers

and the black whips of our hair, past our brothers
in visors and cut-off football tanks, lost in the long
switchgrass and dewy goose shit.
And our mothers raced! Piggybacking frilled babies

over the grass to catch butter cookies
strung on a white finish line with their teeth,
to the slow opening and closing butterfly thighs
of their men. Far from the dented Volvos and Hyundais

left in the parking lot, these husbands whirled and spun
like dervishes around that imported leather rugby ball
from Seoul, bathed in a halo of their own sweat
and kicked-up dirt. Our parents gathered,

shook loose the work day, their hangook tongues
like wild geese skimming over a cool lake.
They popped open barrel-shaped Budweisers
and let the foam spill over.

My father tilted the can to baby Sarah's mouth
and laughed at her sputtering, a laughter so serious
I think I forgave him, his hungry, rough cheeks stilling
to the woman's hungry, rough songs. And Jung Yun's uma

sang like a torn-up hymnal. She sang until
we dropped the twigs and pigeon feathers from our hands
to sit cross-legged in the nests of our mothers, voice as cracked
as the dishes flung over our heads in our kitchens,

she sang like a yanked-out phonecord; shrill,
cut, and ringing, she sang like doves, like elephants
we'd imagined but never seen, she sang a temple
over our upturned faces,

a '70s pop ballad fervid with religion
so unlike our Sunday falsettos.
She sang, and we believed in a smaller,
gruffer, chip-toothed god; she sang the dusk down.

And we, staring up at her knees,
rested in the blue fall of each others' shadows
while the bap and ban chan, paper plates and water coolers
were left, for once, gratefully unattended.

## New Year's Eve

Because of snow, none of the five
cab companies — Phoenix, Bushwick,
Four-Twos, Arecibo, or Priscilla —
answers the phone. Street empty.
Three wine coolers, and I hit the roof.

Nelson, curled into covers,
restrings his boots and lugs two chairs
upstairs. He unlatches the top door
jeweled with ladders, paint rolls, and brushes,
pushes it into snow so thick — bluewhite — it seems a sin,
and just that pleasurable, to insult it with steps
decisive as Hollywood handprints.

Before us, a city connecting cold rooftops.
St. Barbara's shadowed bell strung with light,
skyline through a skein of thin branches.

Corona tilted in a cave of snow.
We can't see the digits on his beeper
signalling the next millenium, but we hear it,
announced in the music of fireworks,
sirens rattling down Linden.

Through our ice-matted boots, I hear it,
the brrakka brrakka so close we both duck, bullets so close
their echo resounds like a caveblast. Unromantic, now,
the silhouette of a man two blocks away
plugging his .44 upwards, each shot
marked by a small cloud rising.

I want to leave, but feel the heat skimming through my organs
and like it. Nelson wants to call Nicky to check if he owns
a spare. We remain standing, necks craned, alert as gazelles,
witness to the shot poem — dangerous,
seething with the fury of stark canvas,
blank paper.

On a cold rooftop
against the scaffolding of January,
we stare up at the sky
for what furious gifts await us.

# Notes

p. 15 - First line from Pablo Neruda's poem "Tus pies [Your Feet]."

p. 33 - Ideas and lines adapted from *Guidebook for Marines*, 16th revised edition. July 1990. Pub. 04. Marine Corps Association, Quantico, Virginia.

p. 71 - Italicized quotes taken from or inspired by a documentary by Yong-ju Byun about comfort women entitled "The Murmuring" (90 min, 16 mm, 1995).

p. 82 - "You your best thing" from Toni Morrison's *Beloved*.

# Acknowledgements

Grateful acknowledgement is made to these publications, where some of the poems (or earlier versions of them) first appeared:

**Barrow Street:** "Queen Min Bi"
**The Best American Poetry of 2003:** "Queen Min Bi"
**Century of the Tiger:** "Ode to the Picnic Singers"
**The Cream City Review:** "Culebra Revisited"
**Glimmer Train:** "Korean Lullaby"
**Icarus:** "Meat Trucks"
**Koream:** "Sa-I-Gu"
**Manoa:** "House of Sharing"
**Monday Night:** "Marine Rules," "Lions"
**The Northridge Review:** "Rosaries"
**Roots and Culture:** "Steven Outside the Fish Store"
**The Sarah Lawrence Review:** "Culebra Revisted"
**Tea Party:** "Jejudo Dreams"
**Watchword:** "Turtles"

I would also like to thank The Asian American Writers' Workshop, The New York Foundation for the Arts, WritersCorps, Youth Speaks, Hedgebrook, and the Serpent Source Foundation for their support.

Deepest thanks to my community, family & friends:
Sucha, Chan Yoo, Sunwoo, Hyunwoo, Hyunjee, Ui Sun, Hyo Sun, Uncle Joe, the Park & Yi families, Mabel Tso, David Velez, Anmol Chaddha, Pimpila, Jeannie, Edward, Anantha, Quang, Taiyo, Kai, Malaya, Mas, Nancy, Beau, Omar, Eric Gamalinda & Eileen Tabios, Kaya, FeedBack, Kyu & Peter, CreateNow, CAAAV, Bar 13, KEEP, Kearny Street, Locus, Jamaesori, Global Talent, Speakout, Steve Cannon, Regie Cabico, Lisa Yun, Bamboo Girl, Zola, Hisae, Sze Pui, Llane, Yoel, Ariel, Bassey, Amalia, Suheir, Junot Diaz, Martín Espada, Suzanne Gardinier, Regina Arnold, Chikwenye Ogunyemi, William Kelly, Alex Chee, Elaine Kim, Kim Addonizio, Jeri Chevalier, Sesshu Foster, Janet McAdams, Dennis Kim, Jee Kim, Megyung, Tina, Richard, Rain, Pat Rosal, Jane Kim, David Huang, David Oh, Bao, Ed, Giles, Chamindika, Sheng, Itzolin Garcia, James Kass, Chinaka, Mei-Lei & M'Kai, Bamuthi, Eddy Zheng, Yuri Kochiyama, Little Nelson Abreu & family, Sunyoung & Julie — **saranghe.**

## About the Author

Photo by Emmy Park

Ishle Yi Park is a Korean American woman born in New York in 1977. A recipient of a fiction grant from the New York Foundation for the Arts, her work has appeared in numerous publications, including *New American Writing*, *Beacon Best Writers of All Colors 2001*, and *The Best American Poetry of 2003*. Ishle has performed in the United States, Cuba, and Korea, and she was a featured poet on HBO's *Def Poetry Jam*.

www.ishle.com.